Growing Up
In Mechanicsville

Disclaimer:

• The sample scenarios in this book are fictitious. Any similarity to actual persons, living or dead, is coincidental.

• This book does not replace the advice of a medical professional or therapist. Consult your physician before making any changes to your diet or regular health plan.

This book is dedicated to my mom, Mrs. Betty Hines - 1/13/1941-3/22/2015. Thank you for the encouragement you gave me. Even when I was down, needing someone the most, you were there. You taught me how to read and write, expecting greatness out of me. And to my children, Amanda, Keesha, Keith, and Christopher, thank you for loving me unconditionally - as well as those who have believed in me throughout every step.

You all saved me.

-Thank you.

Watching It All
From My Window's Reflection

A young girl, who most would call talented at her age, sat by the threshold of her window, looking down at the busy streets below.

She was engaged.

She imagined herself prancing around in the streets, meeting anyone who inhabited the vast arena out there.

Everyone was an individual in her world.

Even so, she couldn't help but admire a world far outside of her own. Gazing across the active streets below was her antidote to boredom. Living in a small apartment near center of Atlanta, GA, it was expected to be anything but quiet, and she was not disappointed.

During the day, people and cars flooded the streets, filling the atmosphere with chatter and honking. But it was during the late hours of dusk when the real magic happened. The glistering city lights took the stage during the night, giving way for performers and dancers to crowd the street, entertaining all who passed by.

The little girl loved it. She loved seeing the expressiveness of the streets below. Her mother, however, was much less of a fan. She opted to drag the girl from the window when caught there, educating her on the dangers of the world outside.

The little girl didn't mind, though. Her two-year-old mind could only comprehend the innocence of the outside world, leading her to understand that the window she loved was an escape to her utopia.

Despite her mother's warnings, she continued to sit by the window - but she had to be crafty with it. During the night was her favorite time, so she'd wait until her mother was asleep then climb up to the threshold of the window.

She sat her eyes shut, listening as the streets sang her to sleep.

At last, she was home.

I Remember a Time..

I remember sitting at the window, gazing across the active streets below. We lived in a fairly small apartment near the center of Atlanta, GA, where it was anything but quiet.

I loved it, though.

I was only two at the time, but I felt as if I were on top of the world, watching it run from the window's reflection.

During the nights, I would climb up to the threshold of the window seal, gazing at the glistering lights as the streets sang me to sleep. I was at peace there.

My mother was opposed to this, though. She would often tell me to stay away from the window, as it wasn't the safest place around.

Betty is what everyone knew her by. She was a strong, tactical woman in every way imaginable. Her beautiful, dark skin absorbed every eye that glanced at her, complimented by her furled, thick hair. I was the youngest out of her five children, so she was the most protective over me, and for good reason too.

By the time I came along, there was already trouble and war brewing in the family. From the moment that I was born, I had the silver spoon of luxury snatched from my mouth. The fissure had already been created between everyone, and I was left in the center of it all.

It was a rare sight to see us all come together, which was often during unfavorable moments.

I was sitting on the window seal, minding my usual business, gazing at the street, when the phone rang. I never answered the phone. That was Mom's job. I continued street gazing. Mom eventually came within the fifth ring and answered in her soft, stern voice. Within an instant she let out a chilling scream. It was a scream unlike anything that I've ever heard before. I was frozen with panic seeing my mother drop to the floor, crying and screaming with the phone clutched to her heart.

My oldest brother, James, had passed away.

The screams of pain filled by the tears of a heartbroken mother is an image that could fill any mind with sorrow. It's a fear that every mother has. The fear of losing their child.

My mother wasn't exempt from this, in fact, she was a victim of it. Her oldest son had passed away due to a car crash on September 15th, 1975. Understandably, everyone was in a trans-like state of disbelief from the news. There was a numbness in our hearts that could not be filled, though the release of emotions helped lessen the pain.

I was more than concerned, though. Up until now, I had never seen my mother like this. From my point of view, I hoped that I never would again.

The funeral was held a few days later. An inside joke within the family was that the only way we would come together in unity was in moments of sorrow.

That joke proved to have significant weight to it.

The morning of the funeral, I sat by the window admiring the streets when Mom walked into the room. She didn't drag me from the window as she usually did. Instead, she picked me up and embraced me with a hug before carrying me outside to the funeral home.

The funeral went as well as anyone would expect. Cries filled the air. Despair took a presence in the home. I felt the grief of everyone - and the presence of another. From the corner of my eyes, I watched as a man continued to stare in our direction. The man was well dressed and carried a sense of intimidating class, which fogged the thick air.

I didn't know what to do, so I grasped onto Mom's dress for the remainder of the service, occasionally peeking to see if he was still gazing in our direction.

After the funeral service, it was time to head to the burial grounds to lay James to rest. A shiny, black limo was parked outside, where everyone gathered to catch a ride there. Mom and I were the first to enter the vehicle. We took our seats closest to the window. By this point, I was fascinated. I tilted my head up out of the window, gazing at the large buildings surrounding them. To me, these seemed to stretch a million miles into the sky.

I was mesmerized by this world, from both above and leveled ground.

I held Mom's hand as we waited, which is where I felt the safest. I continued to twirl my feet with a sense of nervous excitement, gaining a feeling of urgency as time went on. Mom held a facade of courage, with the occasional tear shedding from her eyes. It was apparent that these tears came from a grieving heart.

The limo door swung open, starling us both. From the outside, a man, a woman, and a child all climbed into the limo, taking a few seats adjacent from us.

I clutched Mom's hand even more.

It was the same man as before. Mom didn't pay them any mind, though. She continued to hold a face of courage, opting to look out of the window, instead. Regardless, I still peered around the limo, holding my best face of courage as well. I was set to prove that I, too, could be strong - just like my mother.

The limo left shortly after, proceeding to the burial grounds. The funeral concluded after we said our final goodbyes.

It was a bitter day...

In more ways than one.

..When My Name Changed

As soon as I could remember, Mom encouraged me to begin reading and writing. She was heavily passionate about this because, as a child, she did not get these opportunities - which led to her becoming illiterate in that area of her life.

This had a significant impact on her. I understood where mom was coming from, though, so I began educating myself by first learning how to read and spell my name, Christann.

It wasn't too long after that I began taking frequent trips to the library. I would often stack thirty or more books above my head, creating a mount of knowledge. I grew a love for reading and would often imagine what it would have been like to be one of the greats. Legends of my time filled the lines of most books I read, gracing the pages with praise from their significance in the world.

Deep down, I knew that I was no different. I could be someone great, too.

At the age of five, I began school. The new laws against segregation were still pristine at this time, so things were changing around the city.

I was introduced to my teachers, Ms. Smith and Ms. George, who, to my despair, weren't the most lenient people in the world. Regardless, I tried my best to succeed. I couldn't help but feel a sense of irony that my name was the biggest challenge for everyone to grasp. At one point, I felt myself teaching people how to say my name more times than I did studying. Chrisann (Chris-Sann) was the name my mother gave me. She wasn't sure how to spell most things, so she gave me what she could.

And how I loved it. My teachers, however, were less than enthusiastic about it.

They made it their secondary mission to express their detest for my name, telling me it was incorrect under their ruling. Because of this, my name, Christann, had now become Christina - for their convenience.

Under this name, I felt as if I were a brand new person.

Although, that would prove to be true as I developed-

Under certain circumstances...

at least.

The Perfect Rambler

The Perfect Church. In the name of a new era of Christianity, what seemed like gold on the outside was less than a cheap imitation on the inside. The Perfect Church was more than a social gathering - it was a lifestyle. One that was extremely inclusive to those who would follow their ideals.

They seemed to have the puzzle pieces of my life all in order. All figured out - just like my mother. The Perfect Church was an astounding part of my early life, influencing various factors ranging from where I lived to how my childhood would play out.

My clothing proved to be a prime example of this. I didn't dress like other children, bestowing bright, free clothing. Instead, long, dim dresses flooded my body each day, complimented by my daily crown, a turban. Mom was adamant that this clothing style, as it helped us blend in with the church.

I wasn't too big of a fan, though. I was never one to accept the heavy burden of rules forced into my sponge-like brain. The fear factor of both Heaven and Hell was used to control my actions. If my heart said that something was right, but the church disagreed, then I was automatically classified as the wrong and rebellious. Unintentionally, this attitude followed me into my daily life, shaping me into the person I was proud to be. A sunny morning chirped, allowing me to enjoy my frosted flakes with nature's choir in the background. To keep myself occupied, I began reading the back of the milk carton.

Another missing child.

Among many, these haven't been new, or surprising, stories to me. I had become desensitized due to the amount that I hear. They were everywhere - but unless that was your child, it was unlikely anyone would put forth immediate, lasting action.

I remember analyzing this milk carton, trying to make sense of the face.

Mom walked up to the table and hugged me. She pulled the carton from my grasp and began telling me the newest happenings in the church.

"You know," she began.

"There's a lot of people who need help in this world. I want to be there to help people. I want to be there for you, too."

She placed the carton down and sighed.

"There will be someone staying with us for a bit. A couple of people moved into town and need a place to settle for a while."

I was ecstatic with this news. I would have a new friend at home to spend time with. Mom and I spent all week preparing for our new guests. We cleaned and cleaned, emptying out space for them to stay comfortably. I helped as much as I could. I wanted to make the best first impression possible.

There was an obstacle, however. A big, orange one.

In the living room sat the monster - a big orange couch. I was never a fan of it and made that clear to Mom every chance that I got.

"Mom! We have to get rid of it. It's ugly and-"

"Don't start," she exhaled.

"Fine."

I scrunched my nose and trotted to the other side of the room. I watched as mom dusted the couch and creased the edges with her hands. From what I could tell, she thought it was the perfect addition to our home. It made her feel complete.

I didn't have much time to rebel against the decision - because today was the day.

The day that our new guests would arrive.

Journal 1, Entry 4:

Another Side of a Girl

The catalyst to a world of trouble.

Ultimately, these were the positions that I placed myself in. Although, sometimes, unknowingly. It began with my rebellious attitude toward my clothing. I loathed the long, dark dresses. I loathed the air tight turban. I loathed it all - especially when I had to wear that to school. I was teased by the students - even teachers on occasion due to this.

All hope was not lost, though. I had a plan.

A while ago, Mom and I had went shopping at the Salvation Army for clothes. There wasn't anything too special until I saw it. It glistened like gold and shined like diamonds in my eyes. It was perfect for me. A blue-jean outfit. I snatched the outfit off of the shelf and ran to Mom, begging her to buy it for me. Though it wasn't something we would usually wear, she agreed since we had the extra funds - but on one condition.

"You will not wear this outside of the house. Not to school, and especially, not to church - you hear?"

I nodded frantically. I was willing to tell her anything that she wanted to hear if it meant that I could come one step closer to getting that outfit. We bought the outfit and it has been stored away ever since.

I ran to my closet and dug through the arsenal of

dresses and shoes until I found it. The bright jean outfit. I gasped with excitement and hugged it. Mom was clear on her instructions. I could get in big trouble if I was caught, so I made it a priority to be extra cautious.

Mom left for work before I went to school and didn't come home until after I finished school. This was the case most times. The perfect window of opportunity was handed to me. This was my time to wear the outfit. Later that morning, I threw on one of my usual gowns and waited for Mom to leave.

"Alright. I'm heading to work. Be careful, as always, and I love you."

"I love you too, Mom."

I waited a few moments after she closed the door. I didn't want to be in too much of a hurry - avoiding careless mistakes. After I knew for certain the coast was clear, I hopped off the couch and changed into the outfit for today.

The outfit was my dream. It changed how I felt about myself.

This was my Cinderella dress.

The Flow of Trouble

A few days of wearing the outfit gave me all of the confidence in the world. According to myself, THIS was the person I was always meant to be. I was finally able to express myself.

People noticed me for all of the right reasons this time. The bullying slowed down, and I was happier.

Well - while it lasted.

I pranced home in my jean outfit, reminiscing the amazing time I had today. I skipped up to the door and took a deep breath, turning the knob. I opened the door and glanced around a bit before standing pale to what was in front of me.

Mom.

She came home from work early that day to surprise me. I was surprised - but not in the best way. She looked at me up and down, with my jean outfit on, and was filled with disappointment.

"Now, I already told you - you know what. Never mind."

She escorted me to the back room and retrieved the outfit, punishing me in the process.

The next day was dreadful for me. I was stripped of my outfit - my Cinderella dress, and was sent to school in my usual dim dress and turban. The bullying at school soon picked up again, too. Everyone made fun of my clothes and gave me constant trouble because of it.

I was angry.

I was hurt, but I was also ready to step up this time.

I began to threaten the bullies, telling them what would happen if they continued to pick on me. That didn't stop some of them, though, so I had to resort to violence. The ones who continued received my full wrath, causing me to get into many fights. Eventually, the school had enough of me. After a long decision making process, I was ultimately removed from the school. Mom was not too happy with this decision. She tried to fight it - but was shut down.

A few weeks later, I was set to go to Dunbar Elementary, which wasn't the best school for me. They were the only ones to accept me, though, so I did not have a choice.

I was ready to begin again; holding my breath as I anticipated the future ahead of me.

The Sound of Growth

Womanhood has always been a sensitive topic for the world. A confusing one, too. On one hand, we are taught that women are a strong, powerful species of human, ready to tackle the world around them. But on another hand, we are taught that women are placed here as servants, dedicating their lives for the validation of male needs. The Perfect Church was a heavy advocate for the latter, often dismissing full gender equality one way or another.

As for myself, there seemed to be no excuses for my rebellious attitude against this topic. For all I knew, I was just me. That was more than okay.

Mom was on the fence with most things, though, including this topic. She felt that women were strong and powerful, but due to her upbringing, she had an obligation toward following what The Perfect Church said and did.

As I began to grow into my body, my mind became more curious to the topic of womanhood. Was I meant to be as the church said? Or was there more to my upbringing than I was led to believe? I found myself searching for answers more often than not, using any excuse to learn more about this fascinating world around me.

One of my favorite sources was an old radio that Mom kept hidden from me. Whenever she went to work, and I came home from school, I would find the radio, dash away to a safe space and turn it on. The beautiful sound of music marinated in my ears. I could imagine myself dancing to the rhythm. I could imagine myself as the star of a show, commanding my backup dancers with the rhythm of my graceful movements.

Just like my window, this was my escape from the world. I loved hearing the various stories on the radio, too. I tuned in to get the next big scoop of the day. Whether it be crime, inspiration, or just laughter, I always felt involved - as if I were part of the conversation, too.

I had a voice here. One that finally mattered.

The Back Side of An Experiment

The house was crowded this time around. More people had moved in with Mom upon The Perfect Church's request. I didn't mind this. I loved meeting new people at this stage of my life. There was always something new to learn about my surroundings. I loved it.

I woke up from my bed and stretched. The birds chirped today, giving the bright, morning sun a handsome greeting.

I loved days like these.

Getting up from bed, I was careful not to make too much noise, as I did not want to wake our new guests.

I composed myself just as a ballerina would, dancing around the house on my toes to avoid making too much noise. I was stealthy and quick, which worked to my advantage. I made it past the guest rooms and into the kitchen.

I was starved from a night full of dreaming and rest.

My attention darted towards the Frosted Flakes on the counter, eying them just as a tiger would its next meal. I paced over and hugged the box tightly, whispering various phrases I've seen from animal channels on T.V.

"I got ya! You're mine, you rotten prey!"

Breakfast went the same as it always did these days.

Although, I found a new child on the milk carton this time. This was always a somber view for me - to see someone who was so young be put into situations like this.

"Don't worry, I'll be able to help - someday," I whispered.

I finished my cereal and began to clean my mess. From behind, a loud, dragged out yawn startled me. I turned around thinking I had woke Mom up by mistake, but I was relieved to see a different face. It was our new guest. My new friend, Karen. When Karen and her mother moved in, we instantly became the best of friends. Although she was a lot older than me, I practically saw her as a sister. We had so much in common. During school nights, she would help me study. During the weekends, though, we would play games. Any game ranging from hide and seek to chess we enjoyed.

One of these weekends, we were rightfully bored. Karen and I had played every game we owned and spent a lot of time trying to make up a new one. Thats when Karen had an idea.

"I know a game we could play!"

She grabbed my hand and hauled me to my room. I was excited. We finally had something new to play. I asked Karen what we had to do, but became nervous when she gave me this sinister look. It's one that I've never seen before, and although it scared me, I did my best to put on a brave face.

She began undressing.

"We have to take off our clothes for this game."

I was confused. I couldn't understand why we had

to and I didn't want to, so I spoke up.

"Why do we have to? I don't want to."

"Stop being a baby and do it!" She screamed.

I was startled, so I did what she asked, regretfully. Karen came over to me and hugged me.

"I play this game all of the time. It's really fun and you'll enjoy it."

We played our game. My tears and pain were a symbol for this day. I was hesitant to forgive myself after. I felt disgusted with myself, saying that I could've done more.

I could have been the one to put a stop to things right there, but I didn't.

I was overridden with fear.

I complied, so does that make me the bad guy? Does that make my consent invalid?

Karen forced me to play the special game with her every chance that she got. When I refused, she threatened to tell Mom and the church how I had sinned - how I made Karen do terrible things. I felt stuck and complied with her. I became numb to the feeling as if it were a part of my body. I had racing thoughts and nightmares constantly. I felt as if this was my fault for partaking in these actions.

I knew that it was wrong, but at that point, I didn't care.

Maybe this is who I am.

Maybe this is who I was meant to be.

The Eye of the Beholder

As the days came and went, the dissatisfaction of life plagued my brain and body. I was yearning for excitement, something to change my life for the better. After Karen influenced my life, I became more ruthless than ever, unintentionally pushing people out of my life due to my insecurity of a blunder-filled life.

I opted to turn to something, anything, that could influence my life for the better.

When I was able to receive any money, I ventured out to the local corner store. This was the place for most of my go to needs. Food, necessities, and whatever you could name, it was here. One thing that peaked my interest were the magazines. Playboy was the world's go-to these days. I was curious as to why. I picked one up and shoved it between the bread and eggs that Mom had instructed me to get. I was nervous to check out with this magazine, but I just knew that I had to satisfy my curiosity at any cost.

I walked up to the cash register and paid. The cashier gave me a look but brushed it off due to the sake of business. These magazines weren't cheap, after all.

I paced home with the groceries in my hand, excited to see what I had been missing out on. I hopped through the door, set he groceries on the counter and scurried to my room. The magazine was in perfect condition. The crisp edges were complimented by the glossy structure of the cover. The smell of plastic filled the room as I opened the magazine. I was in awe. There were so many beautiful women in here. Thin bodies with blond hair and blue eyes, too. They were graceful, beautiful and wealthy. Things that I always wanted to be more of.

They were the height of the country. The American standard.

I searched my way through this magazine each day, pretending I was the person they were. I became addicted to this feeling, eventually venturing out to the store - buying more, and more.

I kept these magazines stored under my mattress. I didn't want Mom to find out because I knew that she would see these as wrong.

Still, though, I enjoyed looking at these magazines and people, comparing them to the voids that filled my world.

The satisfaction of my womanhood was met with these fantasies throughout my imagination.

Although my reality showed me something different, that didn't matter. I was happy here.

Hotline Blues

Communication has become a key factor in multiple areas of the world. From speaking to obtaining a letter, there seemed to always be a way to effortlessly communicate with someone. This was apparent with the newest advancement of communication within the last century, phone lines.

Mom had a phone line at the house - used to communicate with the church and work. The line was scarce, so I barely had the chance to touch it - not that I had anyone to call, anyway.

Still, the phone was amusing to me. I had the chance to reach someone miles away at any moment.

One time, as I sat in my room looking at the magazines, I saw an ad placed for a phone chatline. The ad didn't describe it as much more than "A Chatline For The Brave And Bold."

Judging by this description, I was the perfect fit. According to myself, I was both brave and bold.

I scrammed from my room and into the kitchen where the phone sat.

The white phone hung its coiled tail down the wall. I took a few deep breaths before picking up the phone. I put in the number, accessing the chatline.

I didn't know what to expect when I was getting myself into this, but it sure wasn't what I experienced. Loud voices clogged the phone, rambling one after another. I tried speaking up the best I could but was easily overshadowed by the amount of powerful voices there were.

I hung the phone up with heaps of anxiety washing through my body. My fingers were shaking and my body felt the adrenaline rush camping inside of me.

I was scared - but I also felt accomplished.

Over the next few days, I gained the courage to enter the chatline each day to see the different talks going on. Eventually, I gained the courage to begin speaking. I spoke to all kinds of people from both near and far. All types of life stories became the highlight of my days. Throughout the weeks to come, I found and made friends here. I loved seeing a place where people could interact and be themselves in this world.

Mom put an end to this, though. One evening, she came to me with a paper in her hand. She proceeded to drag me to the phone and shoved the paper in my face.

It was a bill.

A three-hundred dollar phone bill.

She banned me from using the phone from that day forward and sent me to my room. Although I was upset at first, I couldn't help but take full responsibility for my actions...

...Eventually, at least.

Stage Freights, Light Nights

I shook in my boots. My fingers cramped and my hands clammed. My vision became skewed, altering the perception of everything in my line of sight. My body was soaked with heat, apparent by the amount sweat that could drown a city.

I was nervous.

Days earlier, I came across a theater group at school. The Crackers is what they called themselves. Why? I'm not entirely sure - but they looked entertaining nonetheless. To my surprise, everyone was extremely welcoming, embracing me with open arms. I was quickly given a script and role to play, then the rest became history.

This became my newfound hobby.

Outside of class and studies, I spent most of my time preparing for my role. Since the group was scarce on members, I had a lead role - meaning a LOT of lines. Day by day, though, I memorized each one. These soon became second nature to me.

I danced around in my room, imagining that I was the star of the show, singing my lines the best I knew how.

I was there, again, in my happy place. Nothing could stop me here because I was the ruler. The queen. The star of my world.

Backstage, I took a few deep breaths. I talked

myself down the hill, even if I was ready to jump - not knowing what awaited for me at the bottom.

The rest of The Crackers came to me and assured me that everything would be more than fine . We were a team. We couldn't let one another down.

I'm not sure if that was the push that I needed, but it worked. I was up and ready to give it my best shot. I took more deep breaths, tilting my head towards the ceiling with a smile.

"I got this!"

I patted my face, and rushed to the bathroom, making sure my costume was still in tact.

Thankfully, it was.

Roll call began on stage. I lined up in my position, ready for the play to begin. At the flick of a switch, the curtains began to soar in the air, allowing the audience to get a full view of the cast on stage. Most of the seats were full, except the one I reserved for Mom. She never showed up. She had to work. Still, I imagined her sitting there with a smile on her face - one that resembled a proud parent.

A proud guardian angel.

The play came to an end later that evening and we were met with a roar of applause and whistles. Everyone lined up and took a bow for their Oscar worthy performances. I stood there as the stage lights shined in my face. I was stunned by the amount of support and cheers we received. I took a bow, holding back my tears from sprouting out.

I did it. I was finally a star...

One that no one could see.

Journal 1, Entry 11:

The Runaway

Rash mornings are bound to happen some days, making it difficult to bounce back at times.

That was the case for this specific day.

Tensions were high this morning. Mom and I had argued plenty of times, but never like this. Something was just different. She came to the kitchen, and snatched her purse from the counter. I sat there and continued eating my Frosted Flakes. There was nothing to say to her - nothing to do. She left shortly after in silence, allowing me to sound a sigh of relief.

"Finally," I mumbled.

Things were tense ever since we made a visit to the clinic. A traumatic experience for the two of us. One that could've been prevented if I had made smarter moves.

At the clinic, I was told by Mom that this sin against God was to remain between both her and I. Although it was against our wishes, it was better for my future to be maintained this way.

We walked in the clinic, trembling due to the fearful sets of judgmental eyes in the walls. My immediate thought was that we didn't belong in this place. At my age, we shouldn't be here for me. I made a mistake, and now I had to reap the consequences.

I was called to the back by the nurse. I trembled

with fear, hoping for a miracle within time. I wanted to go back into the past. If I knew I could have prevented this, I would have.

The procedure went smoothly...well, at least as smooth as it could've gone. I felt disgusted with myself after. I've always been told that the sin I committed would live on in me for eternity. I was scared, but continued to put on a brave face for Mom. I knew she was afraid, too. Afraid of what people and others would think if they ever found out what we had done.

It had been weeks since I went to the clinic. Mom and I still had tension spreading around one another. Sometimes, we would go the entire day without speaking a word to the other. I wasn't used to this treatment, but I adapted. I couldn't help but feel that this could've been avoided.

I had the chance to make smarter decisions.

I finished my cereal and washed my dish in the sink. It was almost time for me to catch the bus to school. I gathered my bag and belongings then headed out of the house.

The windy atmosphere set the mood for that morning. It was chilly with bursts of heavy winds flowing past me, tangling with my hair as I stood there waiting for the bus.

The bus was late today - per usual. It might have been the city traffic, but I could bet any money that the bus would never be on time. The bus finally arrived and I boarded it with ease. Most of the seats were taken, so I made my way to the back of the yellow bus. My slow, rocky walk was taken aback by a few people. I was nervous, so I gazed around frantically looking for a seat.

"Do you need to sit?"

The voice startled me. I looked down the isle to see someone standing up. He gestured me over and I quickly sat down.

"I saw you were looking for a seat, so I thought you could sit here."

I smiled and thanked him. He returned the favor by smiling back, showing the set of perfect teeth he had. His smile was a warm one for me. There was something charming about him that I couldn't quite tell. Either way, I was happy. I had a seat now.

The bus pulled up to the school and I began to gather my belongings to exit.

"It was nice to meet you ..um.."

"It's Christann."

I rose from the seat and headed out of the bus, I didn't want to be late for class. I couldn't afford another mishap for today.

The day went by fairly quickly. I was able to stay focused, not letting my nerves about the clinic take over me.

I opted to walk home this time. I needed the fresh air to clear my head and thoughts. Sometimes, I felt as if I were a complete failure, having the need to constantly depend on people to survive. I wanted things to be different.

I wanted things to change.

I kicked the pebbles on the sidewalk thinking about the world out there. It was always shown to be so vast, yet I was confined to this one place. I wondered what else was out there for me to see. What else was out there for me to discover? The next day started out the same. Mom wouldn't speak to me and I left for the bus shortly after. Upon boarding the bus, I immediately saw the person from last time. He gestured me over with a smile and I took a seat.

"It's Brent."

I looked up at him with confusion.

"What?"

"My name. It's Brent. You gave me your name before, but I never gave you mine."

He flashed his smile at me, and I began to blush with enthusiasm.

"Well, it's nice to meet you, Brent."

"Likewise."

The days to come after became a pattern for me. On the bus, Brent and I chatted for a bit before I would head into school. I did find it odd, though, that Brent never came into the school. In fact, come to think of it, I've never seen him around the school...ever. Just on the bus.

Each time I'd ask him, there seemed to be an endless pool of excuses that he would pull from. One day it would be that he forgot his bag. Another would be that he couldn't go very far - and so on.

Eventually, I just gave up. I enjoyed his company. That's all that mattered to me.

I later found out that my best friend allowed Brent to ride the bus with us so that he could see me.

Brent and I had begun spending more time together - even outside of the bus. He would ask me out to different places and we would have a fun time together. All seemed to be heading uphill for once - until Mom found out what was happening.

She became hysterical once I tired to invite Brent over, repeating over and over that he was bad news. I didn't see why, though. From all of the time that I spent with Brent, he showed himself to be one of the most caring guys I've ever met. Mom didn't want to hear any part of it.

"I forbid you from spending time with that boy," she seethed.

My heart was racing. I was panicking. The one good thing in my life was being taken away just like that, as if I had no control over things, yet again.

I rushed to my room wailing tears.

The next morning, I ran out of the house before Mom had the chance to wake up for work. I didn't want to see her at all that day.

I waited for the bus and it eventually came. I found Brent sitting in our usual seat. He bestowed a soft-spoken smile my way. I chuckled with a blush and planted myself in the seat.

The bus ride felt like an eternity. I consciously thought about what Mom said, allowing my mind to spiral in deep thought.

What if she was right? She has always been right. I'm not too sure what to think. She is my mom. Mom's are always correct, right?

Brent patted me on the leg, waking me up from my intense thought.

"Is everything okay?"

I shuffled around in the seat and gave a nervous smile. I knew that I couldn't tell him. That would ruin everything for us - everything for me. When things were going right, they were going wrong. I was never on the winning side, and I was tired of it.

I was old enough. I was human. I could make my own decisions.

I began crying. Tears swelled up causing a grim atmosphere to develop on the bus.

"I can't see you anymore. My mom said she doesn't approve of it."

Brent didn't say anything. In fact, I didn't realize the amount of sinister energy radiating from his presence until I looked up at him. It was something that I had never seen from him. It was scary.

"She said what?"

He had a demonic, stern look on his face. I felt as if he would cut right through me with his glaring stare.

"She said that I couldn't see you anymore. She said you were bad news."

The bus stopped.

Brent stood up and kicked the side of the bus with all of his might and grabbed my arm. He pulled me out of the bus and we began walking the opposite direction of the school.

I squirmed and struggled trying to get answers from him.

"Where are we going? What's going on? You're hurting me!"

He didn't answer, though. Instead, he carried me through the cold, slushy streets of the city.

We eventually arrived a breakfast restaurant down the busy city highway. The people and cars were frantic that morning, barely giving us room to move past. Brent loosened his grip on my arm and began to hold my hand.

"Want to get some breakfast?" He asked.

I was scared and confused, but said yes, anyway. I didn't want to risk making him mad again.

We approached the restaurant and went behind the building. The smell of fresh ingredients filled the air back there. I didn't know what we were doing - but I knew Brent was up to something.

He took off his winter coat and handed it to me.

"Wrap this up and put it under your shirt."

I did as I was told and put his coat under my shirt. It was a tight fit but I managed to do it. Brent smiled and dragged me into the restaurant. He asked for the manager and held me close to him. I felt safe, yet uncomfortable. The manager came to us and Brent began to act hysterical, shedding tears about a heavy subject in his life. He explained to the manager that I was pregnant and we were hungry.

The manager took a look at me and glanced to the kitchen with a signal. He proceeded to nod and guide us to a table in the back.

"This one's on me, folks." He whispered before heading to the kitchen.

I was furious. My face was heating from the embarrassing moment. I wanted to cry, but I was scared that I would make Brent angry, so I kept quiet.

We ate and left the restaurant. I was late. I wanted to head back to school. Brent had other plans, though. He asked me to go with him. He promised to take care of me, and we would live together - having a real family on the way.

I was in awe. Someone finally cared about me in the way I wanted. This was my chance to make my dreams come true.

I finally found my prince charming- or at least, I thought I did.

The Dynamic of New Beginnings

It had been a while since I've been back home. Mom had a search warrant out for me, thinking that I was missing. I was the child on the milk carton. I wanted to let her know that I was okay, but after everything that went down to find me, I was just too scared. Brent was taking care of me now. He was far from the best with his temper, but he knew how to hustle his way around most things. I continued to pretend that I was pregnant to get money and free food from strangers, giving validation to their sympathy. It wasn't an honest living, but it was for the greater good of my future. I dropped out of school for the time being, too. Brent told me that there wasn't a future for me there. According to everything that he told me, he was my future. We spent most of our nights in the streets and shelter. We didn't have a consistent home or system of transportation - because we could never afford to have that luxury. Months went by and I became empty.

I was tired of these cycles.
I was tired of making mistakes.
I was tired of this.
I couldn't express this to Brent, though. I learned my lesson the last time. I still have the marks on my forehead and stomach to remind me. I couldn't forget.

One night, we were out doing our usual thing, begging people to help a 'pregnant' woman on the street. As we entered the inner city, I received a wave of nostalgia that surrounded my heart.

We were in my area.

My home.

We kept walking and I eventually saw Mom's house near the corner. I knew that this was my chance. One way or another, I was going back home.

I had to keep Brent occupied, so I sat down on the sidewalk and told him that I needed a drink of water. He scoffed at me, before reaching to snatch me up. He stopped, though. There were too many people around for him to do anything. He forced a smile on his face and went to the nearby store to get some water.

Once I knew that he was out of sight, I ran. My fight or flight instinct kicked in as I began to pound on Mom's door. Brent came out of the store in a hurry, rushing towards me with a furious look in his eyes. I gave a quick prayer to myself. I was aware that if Brent caught me, I could be taken away again, and most likely lost forever.

I stood at the door as he closed in. A heavy squeaking noise behind me indicated that someone was at the door.

It was Mom.

She was confused and shocked, but I pushed my way inside of the house and slammed the door shut. I proceeded to lock it as she bombarded me with questions. Heavy slams followed the heavy, frantic crying that I was expressing. Brent was kicking at the door shouting various muffled things to it.

Mom grabbed the phone and called the police. Brent was still there pounding on the door. The hinges on the door began to give out - and soon fell to the floor with the rest of the door.

Brent came inside. He was sweating, breathing hard, and in a state of rage. He went to grab me, but Mom stood in between us, telling him to leave.

He pushed her out of the way and she fell onto the ground.

Brent snatched me and we began to walk outside when sirens flashed on the front porch. The police had finally arrived. Brent let me go and began to make a run for it before being caught and arrested.

I ran to Mom, helping her up in the process. She was distraught, but happy to see me again.

A few months went by and we saw Brent on the news. He was being arrested again for a felony charge. I was relieved. This meant that I was unlikely to run into him anytime soon.

A few days had passed.

A few weeks.

A few months.

A few years.

I had grown. I had matured and became a new self once more. I was happy and proud to be me.

That morning, Mom decided to head to the store. It wasn't far, and we needed to get a few things, so I agreed to go with her. We piled up in the car and left.

I loved taking trips like this with her. We had bonded so much that this was a natural occurrence. As we drove in the car, I looked up in the sky. The buildings and the world were still as big as ever.

I loved it, though. This was the world I was in. This is the person that I am.

The buildings began to shrink and fade as we got further away from the city. I could only think about what else was in store for me. I was aware that I had a lot of life left to live, so I didn't want to waste any second of it.

I am ready.

I am - ready.

I - am - ready.

Those were the last words I remember thinking before everything became black. The sound was ominous.

I never knew pure silence could be so loud.

Here I was in my own mind. It was a scary place to be. I couldn't see anything. I couldn't move. The only thing I could do was be present - and still.

After a while, I began to feel a lot of light shining into my mind. The darkness began to lift and I was able to see figures in the distance. They were dressed in all white.

Were these angels?

Was I finally saved from myself?

The distant voices became more clear as time went on.

"She's awake," I heard one of them say.

"Get her vitals," another whistled.

My vision cleared. Hoards of people crowded me. They whispered and spoke in fast tones, making it hard for me to keep up. They held onto me and assured me that everything was okay.

I didn't know who they were, but I believed them.

I didn't have any choice but to believe them, though.
I was helpless right there.

They got me into stable condition. I slept most of
the day, waiting for the medicine to wear off. I woke
up hours later, extremely groggy, trying to remember
what happened.

I began to panic.

I remembered now.

Mom.

I frantically pressed for the nurse, crying out for
my mother. A couple of nurses came in shortly after
and urged me that everything was just fine. They
told me that Mom was in another room. She had a
similar procedure done, and is recovering.

I was relieved.

I calmed myself down, and stared out of the
hospital window. I was back in the city, and the
buildings stood as proud as they ever did. However,
one thing was different. This time, I was on their
level. I could look over the tall buildings from my
hospital room.

I got my wish. I could see more of the world now. I
would've preferred another way to see it, though.

Over the next few days, I reluctantly learned what
happened. As Mom and I were driving, a driver
slammed into the car. We both suffered similar
amounts of damage, with Mom needing a bit more
care due to being older.

I was released from the hospital some time later.
They kept Mom in, though. They said it would be
best for her to recover there. I understood and just

wanted to make sure she was going to be okay.

I visited the hospital every day after that, hoping to take some good news back home with me.

One day, I did - but not in the way I was expecting. I arrived at the hospital for my daily check on Mom. The doctors said she was improving, so that was a nice form of comfort that I received. I was in a hurry today. I had a lot of things to attend to, so I wanted to make the visit quick. As I entered the hospital, a hefty force caused my body to shake and recoil to the ground. I stood up and patted myself down. This was a brand new dress, and now it was dirty.

It was my fault, though.

I was moving too fast.

I lifted my head to apologize and was met with a pair of soft eyes. They stared at me with concern, anticipating my next move. I became flustered.

"I'm sorry. I wasn't looking where I was going. I didn't mean to-"

"It's Keith."

I stared at him.

"Keith?"

"Yes. My name is Keith. It's no problem. You caused no harm."

We blushed and smiled at one another.

Sometimes, I'm thankful for how fate works.

Watching It All
From My New Beginning

I stood there as a young woman, who most would call talented at this age. I sat by the threshold of the window, looking down at the busy streets below.

I was engaged.

I imagined myself prancing around in the streets, meeting anyone who inhabited the vast arena out there.

I was mesmerized.

I envisioned myself taking the world by storm, showing off the person I could be. A big mission to accomplish, I knew - but to me, anything was possible.

I knew from experience.

Large, brown moving boxes crowded the house, making it difficult to maneuver around. Though I had a new life growing inside of me, I did it with little hassle.

Mom was in the kitchen signing release papers. The moving people had come through, so it was finally time.

I rubbed on my stomach. Though it had grown three times as much over the past 6 months, it was worth it. This was the start of a new beginning.

A new generation.

I took one last look at the house. A clean slate awaited elsewhere.

The memories were priceless, though. Each one had a core. Each one had a place in my heart.

I took a deep breath and grabbed my suitcase. I hugged the threshold of the window, thanking it for all of the memories it gave.

Here I was - a brand new person. Outgrowing abuse from my baby sister and uncle, to an abusive relationship with Brent wasn't easy. At one point, Rode vs Wade became my savior.

I took the hits - but I patched myself up.

With one last sigh, and a few tears, I turned off the lights and exit the home.

"It's time for MY new beginning."

Stoney Love
Author/Television Personality

Raised in the urban side of Atlanta, GA, Stoney Love is a character of heart. Although she grew up as Chrisann Hines, with a passion for acting, writing, and entertainment, Stoney developed new passions as she later married, having four children. During that time, Stoney had taken her divorced husband's last name, adopting it as her first name.

Today, Stoney lives out her life as a television and radio host. Her dream of being a storyteller has come to life as she aims to capture the eyes and heart of all who come across her presence.

Earnest Lewis
Author/Publisher

Earnest Lewis is a Canadian-American entrepreneur and bestselling author. He is the founder of the Moonlight Scholars, an organization that aims to give a new light on the known subject of education. Earnest is best known for his writing and publishing skills, releasing over 25 books as of 2022. Earnest is a publisher and a licensed literary agent who aids children in pursuing their proper education.

With the publication of his children's books, Earnest has established a reputation as the "Imagination Activist", helping all reach their full potential in life by opening the door to their imagination. He is best quoted by his phrase "Your imagination is only what you make of it."

Some of his most notable works include The Smallest Roads Are Where Dreams Begin, The Journey of the Little Brown Boy, The Boy Who Brought His Mind to Life, and Beyond the Eyes of A Believer.

In addition, Earnest has substantial prior public relations experience and has worked with numerous clients to diversify their sales channels, create brand awareness programs, and gain more traction for their businesses. He has been recognized and featured in several international media outlets for his achievements as an author.

Thank you.